Tao Te Ching
The Art of Happiness

By Lao Tzu and Dawn Lianna MA

Tao Te Ching

Copyright 2009 by Dawn Lianna MA

All rights reserved. No part of this book may be reproduced in any form, without written permission from the publisher or author, except for the inclusion of a brief quotation in a review or article where full credit is given to the authors.

Editing credits and special thanks to: Kate O'Rielly, Rok Caldwell, Lily Kridelbaugh and Adie Shaw. Many thanks to all the lovely students who have come to listen.

Printed and Distributed by Lightning Source
www.lightningsource.com

Published by Eagle Song Healing
www.laotzunow.com
www.intuitivecallings.com

Cover Design by Carissa Bean
www.designingfresh.com
Library of Congress Control Number: 2009905152

Introduction

The Tao Te Ching has been translated many times. This transmission came through to Dawn Lianna in 2009.

These are messages of love for us for the current times. These messages are simple, profound, poetic and truthful. The words are sweet to the ear and soothing to the soul and help point the way toward happiness.

We sincerely hope you benefit and prosper from these teachings on love, life and the Tao.

"I feel deeply blessed to have Lao Tzu as my guide in this life. For his humble words and light-hearted wisdom, I am very deeply grateful." Dawn Lianna MA

<u>One</u>

What is the Tao? The Tao is life. The Tao is love. Love is the way. Love is the answer. Love is the source inside you. Before the big bang there was formless, unlimited potential. You are part of the manifestation of that potential.

You are made of love. You come from love. In your essence, you are love.

Love

Two

The world you live in is a world of duality. It holds both light and dark. The formless is still here. This reality is really illusion.

Within the illusion is light and dark, good and bad, separation and togetherness.

In your humanness, you are given choice. Which part of the illusion do you choose to focus on? You are also given the choice to move beyond illusion and back to love.

Three

There are many paths. On this earth you live in free will. You make many choices each day. These choices affect what you attract into your life.

You choose your attitude or approach to life. Your choices determine whether you will live in peace and love, joy and harmony, or whether you will take the path of sorrow. Judge not, as both paths come from the same source and both paths are within the same illusion.

However, you came here to enjoy life, the dynamic creation on the earth where beauty abounds. You and humanity are given the choice to live in harmony – or not. Tune in. Be aligned. Allow the source light to feed your soul and bless your life. Make the very best of life. Life is not meant to be filled with false riches, though you may have plenty. The depth of life is in your heart, in your soul. Breathe it in. Breathe in the love in your heart. Do that and be happy in your heart and in your soul. Trust your source. It is eternal.

Four

The source light is within you. It is everywhere. It makes up the substance of all things. The source light is the Tao.

See love in all that you see. Feel love in all that you feel. Hear love in all that you hear. Smell and taste love in all that you smell and taste. That is the Tao.

This source, your source, is your real self. You are the source from whence you come.

Love adores you. The mind creates confusion. Drop down into your heart.

Five

In the center is the Tao. In the center is love. Live life from your center. Take time to connect. Meditate often.

Take time in the morning to look out the window and see the sky. Wherever you are there is a sky. Wherever you are there is your breath. Focusing on one of these two simple things can take you to a place of peace.

Six

The Tao is infinite. Like a mother nursing her baby, the Tao loves you. The Tao is called the middle way. It is the path of balance.

How do you find the path of balance? Through love, of course. Let's make this practical. How do you find balance? How do you find love?

It comes from intention. It comes from the core questions you ask yourself as you move gracefully through your day and your life.

What type of questions will help you stay connected to source, to the Tao? You might ask, "What can I learn here that is of love? How do I stay in love now? What is the source of love communicating to me through this event? How can I remain in a state of love in this moment?"

By staying in your heart, you stay in love. That's it. It's very simple.

Seven

Take care of each other. You are here to enjoy life. If only some enjoy life, life will not be fully enjoyed. If you are enjoying life and your neighbor is suffering, you are suffering. You are one.

Form community. Take care of each other. Learn to love each other as if the other person is yourself. There is really no other. You are already one. How do you take care of each other? You do it by staying in a state of love. Ask yourself, how can I love? Ask your friend and your neighbor, how can I love you or help you?

Then step back and back and back and back and fly above and take the eagle's view. Watch the whole of humanity. Love them as yourself. Then soar down. Go deep into your heart. Your heart is the love pump of your body. Think of someone or something that you love. Let the love flow. Let it continue to flow. Let it generate outward to your closest friends and family. Let it grow. Let it pump out into your community. Let it flow. Let it pump across the earth and back to you again. Let love flow.

Eight

The river of life is flowing. As the water finds its path through the river canal, it flows around all the obstacles. Have you ever seen water get stuck in the river?

Be like the water, still but moving, effervescent and illuminated.

At the ocean you see the waves. They move in and they move out. Have you taken time to think of the bottom of the ocean, the sand underneath the water?

Pass beyond the sand underneath the water into your core. Here you find everything and nothing.

Some say you are inside the universe. It is also true that the universe is inside you.

Nine

Find balance in the middle way. The best life is a simple life, a balanced life. This is life filled with giving and receiving, a life of harmony.

<u>Ten</u>

You are everything and you are nothing. How do you manifest this concept in the world? You do it through humility, of course. When all credit is given to love, you can accomplish great tasks with humility and ease. Love works through you to take your work and your energy into the world.

The clearer you are, the greater your ability to manifest the dream of love through you. Source love is eternally loving. If source love had a longing, it would long only to be more of itself, more love.

Remember your heart is the love pump of the body. It moves the blood through the physical body. It also moves the love. When you give the credit to love, you can do great things.

Eleven

You are everything and you are nothing. This is hard for the mind to grasp.

Go deep within. Notice the animal kingdom. They build their homes. They take their food. They live in harmony with nature and God.

The beaver finds a hole in a log, and drags the sticks to make a beaver dam. Then he lives inside. He has built something of many uses. It protects him. It shelters him and often it is built near or on his source of water. He is busy, but he also knows how to relax. He is comfortable in his humble home. He rests and sleeps in gratitude.

Twelve

You have a choice to make. External pleasures are indeed pleasurable but they bring no lasting happiness. They bring a moment of beauty and a moment of pleasure. This is to be enjoyed. It is part of your life to experience the beauty of nature.

However, there is an inner nature that is so much more magnificent and many have missed it. You have a busy mind, which may keep you from relaxing.

Take time. Go into meditation. Chant the name of God in your native tongue. If you do not believe in God, chant the word love, or the word one, or the word Aum.

Go inside. You will find a magnificent world waiting for you. All is there. And yet there is nothing. This is wonderful.

Thirteen

Say yes to life. When life brings you pleasure, say yes. When life brings you pain, say yes. Fighting life is a useless battle. Surrender to what is. There is power in surrender. The power of grace, the power of life, the power of your inner world, aligns with your surrender.

When you fight what is, you go nowhere. You become the whirlpool that starts to spin and pull you under. Your mind starts to suffer and spin even deeper into your spiral of illusion.

Surrender to what is. When you surrender you let go of the pain and become present. Breathe deeply into your pain and breathe deeply into your joy. The joy will only expand and the pain will cease to exist. Beneath it all is awareness. Be present now to awareness itself.

Fourteen

The Tao is the seen and unseen. The Tao is love and life ever present.

How do we make this practical so that you can understand it? Listen with your heart. Your heart is unlimited. Your heart has no beginning and no end. Can you find an end to the love you feel for your loved ones?

Fifteen

Wisdom comes from love. The wisdom of the one who is in mastery can be seen. This person shows evidence of his or her mastery.

What type of evidence might you see in a master of greatness who is manifesting before you? He or she is peaceful and content, no matter what the outside circumstances.

If he or she experiences desire, the desire moves through the person without attachment. The master is drawn to stillness and lives peacefully.

The master loves to help, but he is not attached to helping or to the outcome of helping. It doesn't matter to the master if he helps many, or if he helps a few. The master is content to simply be.

Does the master get hungry? Does the master experience the desires of the flesh? Yes, of course, the master in form has a belly. His heart is beating. Your body rhythm is just like his.

Sixteen

The ceramic vessel that has water in it is the same vessel as the ceramic vessel that is empty. The vessel that is holding pennies is the same vessel when it is empty.

Your mind holding thought is the same mind when it is empty.

Your heart full of love is the same heart when it is still.

The rhythms of life go on as long as life will go. The Tao is eternal. It is beyond life. It is the substance of all things. It is creator and the created. It is the form and the formless. It is eternal.

Seventeen

Life is illusion, a great superstition. Does that mean you should not enjoy it? No, enjoy your life to the fullest. It's your choice whether you enjoy your life or not.

When you watch a small child who is learning to walk, she takes one step and then another. She does not stop to analyze her steps, she trusts. She moves forward, one moment, one step at a time. When the small child stumbles, she gets right back up and keeps on going. She is in the flow.

Grown people are often not so simple. They sit and analyze what to do. If they are spiritual they may wonder what God wants. How would you know what God wants? How would you find God?

Like the small child who takes one step at a time, move throughout your day, setting one foot in front of the other. You can do this with awareness or you can do it with attitude. I prefer awareness. Awareness of what? Awareness of the Tao. How can you find the Tao? Stay in your heart. Put your awareness on love.

Eighteen

When you are in love things go very well. When things go array go back to love. It is your choice which part of life you focus on.

Even when you are in pain, go deeper through meditation. Go underneath your pain deep within, until you find peace.

Love is always there in your heart, waiting for you, underneath everything else. In fact, it is silly that I even say it is waiting. It is simply there. It is not waiting for anybody. It just is.

Nineteen

The way of the Tao is eternal. The Tao moves through life.

People make choices that are self-evident. They are either moving from love or to love.

Take time each day to go inside and connect with your inner being. This being is neutral. It goes beyond love, into the oneness.

In this place, there is nothing and everything. We are all one. Here desire softens and disappears. What is left when all desire and thought are gone is the Tao.

Twenty

Compare yourself to no one. What does this mean? This means be happy now. Be content with what is. Love what is right in front of you. Love what is in your life.

Longing creates confusion in your mind. When you are already happy and content with what is, you can experience a clean desire. You may be feeling what is coming toward you. Give thanks in advance. This is a powerful prayer. Then go back to loving what is, deeper into what is right now.

Twenty-one

Imagine a thread that runs through life. This thread is invisible but it runs through life anyway.

Imagine a thread that runs through a rug on the floor. It is vital to holding the rug together. Without this thread the rug would not exist. Yet, you fail to see the one thread that is holding the rug in place.

Focus. Imagine that you can see, sense and feel quietly the thread of life. This is the Tao.

Some call it God. Some call it the Universe. Some call it the one with no name. I call it the Tao.

Twenty-two

When you are centered and connected to the divine, your core self, you are happy. Peace exists inside you without any effort. It is there eternally. The peace inside you is already reliable. All you need to do is tap into it and feel its eternal presence.

Peace is always there. It simply is. When you are at peace, you crave nothing. You are humble.

Gratitude is an excellent key to take you through the doorway to the room of peace. Give thanks and the key turns. Give thanks again and the door opens.

Twenty-three

Be still. Go within as often as possible. Go to the reliable place of peace. When you are at peace, you are happy.

Question: "Lao Tzu, what do I do with my desires? Am I not meant to experience them and enjoy life?" Yes, of course you are meant to experience and enjoy life. Being in contact with peace will enhance your life in every way.

This is not a lesson on how to manifest your desire. This is a lesson on how to be at peace.

Be at peace with your desire. See it complete.

Give thanks in advance. Let it go. Go home to love.

Twenty-four

Humility is a key to happiness. Gratitude brings humility. All the goodness of life is a tremendous gift. Live like the sun shines. Live like the moon, reflecting the light of the sun, the light of love.

Let your light shine very brightly but do not boast of this shining light. Give thanks for it. Then your light will shine even more brightly. It is natural. As the light shines and you are happy, you become more humble naturally.

You ask, "How can we be grateful when some are still suffering?" Even the suffering can give thanks. There is an old saying: "I was mad because my foot hurt, then I saw a man with no feet and I gave thanks."

If humanity becomes grateful for the goodness of life, humanity will see the true abundance. They will see that there is more than enough for everyone to enjoy a good life. If humanity is full of gratitude, humanity will share with those who have less. If you radiate more gratitude, you are contributing to the redistribution of abundance and the ending of suffering.

Twenty-five

There is great peace inside your being. This peace is becoming known to many of you. As you get to know the peace inside, it radiates out to the rest of humanity. The deeper your well and your wire tap to peace, the more peace you radiate.

The deeper the well of your love in your heart, the more love you radiate.

Dig a very deep well into peace. Open your heart very wide. Feel compassion for humanity and for your friends. Feel compassion for the so-called enemy. This is compassion for yourself.

Twenty-six

There really is no other. There is no outer world. What you see is a mirror of your inner world. This is very hard for the mind to comprehend.

So how do you live accordingly?

You live according to the Tao. You live according to the energy you feel flowing through your life when you are in tune. You live in peace and harmony and you live with detachment.

Stay present and detached. This creates a connection to a very calm center.

Twenty-seven

Do not expect others to change for you. Change only yourself. Change your thinking, change your thoughts. Go within the deep.

"How do I clear my issues? How do I stop my mind from worrying?"

You stop your mind from worrying through meditation. You give your mind something to pay attention to so you can find the peace.

There are many tools available to you to help you clear issues. These are wonderful tools that have been given to humanity. Use the tools that are appropriate to clear the past from the present. Wipe the slate clean so you can tap into more love and greater peace.

When your issues are cleared, it is easier to tap into the love.

Take care of each other.

Twenty-eight

You live in a world of duality. This is a very beautiful world. It is full of the sun and the moon, the night and the day, the wind and the rain. It is full with light and it is full with the night.

It is full with the waxing and the waning of the moon, the pull of the tides. It is full with cycles that come from the creator.

Though there is this beautiful world of form and beauty all around you, there is also an inner world of the formless. When you are tapped into the formless, there is a great opportunity for peace. When you are in peace, you enjoy the world of form even more.

Twenty-nine

Take time to love. When you are present in the moment, you can access the love in your heart easily. It is always right there. Where you are triggered you are likely to get away from your love. Stop. Breathe. Look at a flower or the sky. Listen to your breath. Go back to the Tao.

Meditation will begin to heal and soften you and help you find the treasures of life. The real treasure chest of life is in the peace of the inner world, in the potential of inner fulfillment.

If you fight the universe you will lose. The universe is much bigger than you are and much stronger. Though you are the universe you are also the individual form. If you are lucky enough to hear the universe, it is best to follow.

Thirty

Surrender to the Tao. The Tao is like a river; it will take you forward in the direction of your dreams and goals. Be peaceful along the way.

If you are on a raft in the river and the river is gentle, you can paddle gently and stay in the middle of the stream enjoying the sunny day. If the river bends and turns, you go with it.

You have dreams, but do not be attached to their fulfillment. You are all right, right now.

Rebellion can take you away from the Tao. You may not choose to conform to all of society's rules and to all of the requests of others. However, too much rebellion takes you away from balance.

Find a balance of give and take, conforming and rebelling, inward and outward movement. Like the ocean waves, go in and go out, like the sun and the moon, shine and reflect, like the summer and the winter, blossom and be colorful, and go inside by the fire.

Thirty-one

Words are neutral. They come in many languages with accents and dialects. Words can be used to help create fear or joy. States of mind create experiences. Experiences are expressed through words.

We experience life. It is your choice which part of life you focus on. Be neutral. Do not judge. When you are neutral, awake and aware, you can find your way through the jungle, the forest or on the beach. If you are neutral, you can find your way alone or in relationship.

Words. They are neutral. Use them wisely to create the experiences you want. Your neurology processes the words you use. Words and people create war and peace. Which one do you want? Create peace.

Thirty-two

Remember the thread that runs through life? Again, I repeat, this is the Tao. The Tao is powerful and yet nothing. The Tao moves by itself. Like a river, when you step inside you feel the water on your legs. When you place your raft on the river, it takes you.

Perhaps you have a destination. You are going downstream to a concert. The river is calm and it is a beautiful day. You can sit down and relax and let the raft take you down the river.

If you fight the river, and try to go upstream, you will have to paddle hard. It will make your body sweat and create stress. If you relax, the river will naturally take you to your clear destination.

Remember the concert? You were clear where you were going. You wanted to enjoy some music. The river will take you.

Thirty-three

When you are present within yourself you are neutral and powerful. You bring your light to the world.

Commitment to your inner self is the first measure of success. Commitment to your inner self is wisdom.

Your intuition is a method by which your inner self communicates with you. It speaks to you of wisdom through your feelings. It communicates with pictures and it talks with no sound.

Thirty-four

Do you feel the bliss bubbling up from inside you? Do you feel the pleasure of knowing yourself? Can you imagine the infinite inside you even deeper than the bliss?

From the infinite came the big bang, the beginning of life as we know it. Before that the infinite potential was unformed. Then came creation. You are part of the creator. You are empowered to create a life, a life of your pleasing and pleasure, or a life of your disaster and hardship. Your choice. What shall you focus on?

Go back to the infinite potential inside you. Then you will know your true self.

Thirty-five

The Tao does not show its greatness and yet its greatness is everywhere.

The wise person drifts inside daily. The wise person takes care of her body. The wise person finds moderation in her diet and in her emotions. When she is tired she rests. When she is motivated she moves.

Remember the river. It drifts. It has times when it is calm and times when the water must go through difficult places. There the water moves quickly and falls over the rocks but it does not tire. It does not stop to complain. It has infinite energy. It is tapped into source. It flows.

The wise person seeks her own counsel and the counsel of wise friends. The wise person seeks the Tao inside.

Thirty-six

Eighty-one names for love. Ninety-nine names for love. One-thousand names for love. What are the forms of love? Ask your heart.

In this world love comes in many forms; the mother for the child, the father for the daughter or the son, the lover for the beloved, the friend for the friend. All the love comes from the same place. All the love comes from the source, the great love source, the source of love. Your heart pumps blood. It also pumps love. When you are attuned to your heart, you are attuned to love.

Your heart is a wonderful place to focus.

Thirty-seven

The world is a place of action. Meditation is a place of non-action. Find balance.

To live a very full life, balance the inner life with the outer life. Live a full life. Follow your heart. Plan your dreams. Live your vacations.

Notice a beautiful leaf. Sit and watch it move in the breeze. Notice the veins in the leaf. They pulsate with fresh life force. Look for the colorful changes on the underside of the leaf. If you watch the leaf long enough it will disappear or you will disappear inside the leaf. You become one.

When you are in the place of the oneness you remain still and peaceful.

You can also do a more active meditation. Visualize your completed desire. Give yourself the satisfaction of gratitude beforehand. Then watch your intention come to you.

Thirty-eight

Become the witness to your own life. Develop neutrality. Neutrality is a choice of focus. Neutrality is a place of being-ness.

Without attachment, life becomes more pleasurable and fun. When you are attached to outcome and the outcome has not yet arrived, you become miserable. You strive and strain and stress. You fill your mind with shoulds and programs. This unsettles you and then you feel off balance.

Return to loving what is. Right now. What is in front of you that you can love? Can you see a leaf from your window?

Thirty-nine

When you go to your heart there is love. Some say, "But, Lao Tzu, my heart is sore and longing. How do I relieve the pain I carry in my heart? My heart has been broken and wounded."

Place your hands above and below your heart in the middle of your chest, near the chakra. Cradle your heart. Send compassion to yourself. Make your hands into a filter. Use the filter to scoop the pain from your heart.

Place the pain that you now carry in your hands out in front of you. See yourself and your loved ones there with you. Send them love. Send love to your families throughout time.

Now, once the love is there, take your breath and blow the image from your palm and send the others away to be loved by their own self. Now return your hands to your heart. Now you can feel the love.

Forty

Heaven and earth bend to the Tao. Heaven and earth were created out of the Tao of nothing. From the formless to the formed, life came forth.

Life is a tremendous gift, meant to be enjoyed. You say, "But, Lao Tzu, there is such joy and hardship here. How do I enjoy hardship?"

I say, breathe. Breathe and ask yourself, How can I love what is right here now? Breathe and the difficult feelings dissolve in the breath. The breath comes from the light. The light is light. Air is light. When you breathe into a feeling, it shifts. It goes neutral. It ceases to be.

When the feeling ceases to be, you are back to the Tao. This is how to enjoy what is. Enjoy life. Live fully. Be happy. Find Balance.

Forty-one

Some people chase after pleasure. They strive and work at life. Some people find pleasure easily and make a lot of money. Some people live in envy of another person's life. How would you know if the person who is rich or poor is happy? What is the true happiness?

True happiness comes from source love. The universe is a very big place. There are all kinds of worlds and stars and planets. You can focus on whatever kind of universe you want to focus on. It is your choice. No matter what universe you find yourself in, you can love. Even when there is stress around you, you can love.

People in developing countries may be lacking in amenities; yet, you might see more smiles on their faces than in a high-class home, where there is no music. Smiles, laughter and fun come from within, from the goodness of your own inner being.

Forty-two

They say laughter is the best medicine. Ha ha ha ha ha ha ha ha ha ha ha ha ha ha ha ha. How long can you laugh? Ha ha ha ha ha ha ha. How long can you take life seriously? Ha ha ha ha ha ha ha ha.

Relieve yourself of your seriousness. Ha ha ha ha ha ha ha ha ha.

Forty-three

I am very happy to be here with you. I am very happy because my heart is wide open. I am very happy to be of service. I am very happy to be connected to love. I am very happy to be in the flow of the Tao. I am content with what is. I am happy to be where I am.

These are the words of a very wise person.

Forty-four

Stay in balance. Do not be attached to outcomes. This will minimize suffering. When you are frustrated, stop. Step back. Go past the driver's seat to a new perspective.

There was a time before this life, when you were in the peacefulness of spirit. Step back, look in.

There is a very thin imaginary veil between yourself and your real self, love. The veil is not really there. The veil is an illusion. It is a word that is likened to forgetting. When you forget the Tao it is like there is a veil between you and the Tao. When you remember, you are the Tao.

Forty-five

A Poem for You

Life is a poem that you yourself write
Life can be pleasure or life can be plight

Love is a river in which you can swim
When you love fully, the river is full to the brim

Sadness come home and sit here with me
I'd rather be happy, at home in a tree

Longing come hither and sit by my side
I remember the ocean has high and low tide

When I am greedy, I am longing the most
When I come home I've nothing to boast

I long for the Tao to come home and feel free
When I am with the Tao, I live life so happily

Forty-six

When you are in turmoil and you are in self-hatred or self-blame, you are in your own self-defeating pattern. You may even know that you are in the pattern but you may not yet know how to clear this pattern. Let's take the things we have discussed so far. Breathe. Breathe more deeply than usual. Breathe very deeply for a few minutes, at least nine or ten big deep breaths.

After you have finished these breaths, focus on your heart. Think of two or three people that you love, that are easy for you to love, maybe a child. Now breathe again into your heart and send love to those people.

Now place yourself out there as a child with those other people. See yourself smiling and full of light. How do you feel now? Are you still in turmoil? "No," you say. "I have reconnected with life, with the breath, with the Tao."

Forty-seven

I am content to just love. I am content to be. When desire rises I follow. If it seems like a good desire, I take action. The Tao moves me to action. I am in tune. The desire is now manifest. I am still in the Tao.

The Buddhists teach to be desire-less. This means to be in your being-ness. To be aware of simple awareness, awareness itself.

"But, Lao Tzu, does that mean don't enjoy my life?" No, you go through life. You experience friends. You go to work. You are with your neighbors. I am referring to how you go through life, how you experience friends, go to work and be with your neighbors. Be gentle, attuned, detached, yet loving and peaceful. These qualities are right inside you. They are sometimes beneath the surface and other times flowing through your life.

Without a body, you can't taste the kiss of your lover or the sweetness of a strawberry. When you are in form, you are meant to enjoy form. Live life fully. Then drop it. Drop it each day, at the beginning, at the middle and at the end.

Forty-eight

The river of life is already flowing and always flowing. When you live in the river of life, you live in the Tao, you live in flow, and you live in a state of love. When you are surrendered the river will carry you. Here you are at peace.

When you try to force the river, it overtakes you. It is impossible to swim upstream for very long or very far.

Relax yourself. In relaxing, you allow life to carry you. This does not mean that you become lazy. This means that you become guided. You move into harmony with the flow of life and life takes care of you, life guides you and life brings you home.

Forty-nine

The main virtue is love. The second virtue is love. The third virtue is love. From love springs humility, tenderness, compassion, reverence and all the other virtues. When you love you are kind. When you love you find your path. When you are on your path, you find love.

It is a great circle, the circle of life. It is a circle of love. You come from love to life and you go back from life to love. Why not go to love now?

It's right here in your heart. Take one or two deep refreshing breaths into your heart and open to the love inside you. This supports the good.

Fifty

When you are here on earth you have a great opportunity. You have a chance to enjoy a life or to destroy a life. Choose life.

Look outside right now and see a beautiful piece of nature. Whether you can see the sky or the ground, a leaf or a flower, the snow or the sun, doesn't matter. See life. See the force behind nature. That is life.

If you are feeling down, remember life. Look out the window or go outside and connect with nature. Find something that is positive and looks beautiful to your eye. Find something that sounds lovely and is beautiful to your ear. Find something with a lovely texture and touch it to your lips. Breathe in the grace of living.

Fifty-one

All things come from the Tao. This means that all things come from love. Love is the key to life. Love is the creator of life. Love gives without giving. Love forms without forming. Love is, and it is always flowing.

Think of a beautiful flower. The flower comes from a seed. Each seed knows its inherent nature. It knows which flower it will become. When you plant a rose, it becomes a rose. It does not become something else. It becomes its true nature.

That is your job as well. Become who you are. You are planted here to be yourself. You are not planted to become someone else. Like the rose who knows its true nature, know your true nature.

You say, "But, Lao Tzu, how do I find my true nature? There is so much interference here. There are so many stories of who I should be and what I should do. How do I know which one to follow?"

continued....

You know which one to follow when you are true to yourself, true to your heart, and true to your soul. You find your heart and soul by listening to yourself.

There are many ways to listen to yourself. You can get very quiet in meditation. You can stop and contemplate quietly, look out into nature or gaze into a candle or fire. You can sit or walk and listen to your own rhythm.

Just like I can't do your stretching for you, I can't tell you how to be or feel. Only you can do your stretching and only you can find your true nature. You find your nature by following yourself, by being true to yourself.

Don't do everything others tell you to do, though you may be polite and loving when given a request. Do what feels right and true to you.

Fifty-two

In the beginning there was light, love, the Tao. You come from the Tao. You come from love. That is your nature. To be loving is to be yourself. Set your good intention to be the love that you are.

Use love when you are speaking your words. Use love when you are cooking your food. Use love when you are driving your car and walking your walk. Use love when you are making love. Love is the source of the energy inside. When you are off balance you are off from love. There are many medicines and ways that can bring you back to balance. The greatest of all is love.

Fifty-three

Stay on your path. Don't get sidetracked. Stay on your path. Be true to yourself. Go the way you want to go, the way you are guided to go.   Go the way of awakening. It is simple. I will repeat myself. Go the way you are guided to go.

Choose what is simple. Stay away from excess. You are better off to choose the path of simplicity if you want to find yourself. This does not mean you cannot have abundance. It means there is plenty for you and plenty for all.

There is enough in this world to take care of every single person abundantly.

Fifty-four

Being true to yourself does not mean to be selfish. You are here in service to love, so you are here in service to others. While serving others, be true to yourself first. Do not give away too much energy. Do not live in excess in any way. Come back to simplicity. Give what feels natural and makes you feel good.

When you are inspired by life, life will inspire you to help others. There will be moments when you are inspired to say yes and moments when you are inspired to say no.

No is as good of an answer as yes, when it is the truth. When no is the truth of your being, it is a better answer than yes.

Listen to what is right for you. Listen to what is right inside you.

Fifty-five

Be like a little child, full of life, full of hope and full of goodness.

Children are usually kind to everyone. They are kind to the worker, the teacher and the cleaning lady. They are kind to the queen and the pauper. They love all. Children believe in the goodness of each person. Children have faith in those around them. Be like the child again.

You too had this innocence when you were young. Where did it go? It is not really very far away.

Use discernment as you come back to the path of trust and service. Take care of yourself. Return to your faith. Have faith in yourself. Accept all parts of yourself. Choose to find the good.

Fifty-six

When you are enlightened you are happy. When you are enlightened you don't care so much about external things. Life for you is simple and you are satisfied.

Like a stone in the middle of the river, life flows around you. You are solid, strong and stable no matter what life brings. You are like a rock.

When you are enlightened you know the steadiness of silence. Your mind is quiet and calm. Inner peace is reliable.

Fifty-seven

Be humble. Live simply. That is all I really need to say to you. But you ask for more explanation. "How do I do that today in the modern world? How do I live simply and stay in a state of love when there is war around me? Why is there war on the planet?"

There is war on the planet because people are out of balance. They are not listening to each other. They are not listening to the true integrity and abundance inside themselves.

They have forgotten their nature is love. They have forgotten that love is ever flowing. They have forgotten that there is enough for all.

So what can you do? First of all listen to yourself. If you are called to be an activist, become an activist. If you are called to become a dancer, become a dancer. If you are called to write, become a writer. Become yourself. Be true to yourself. Share yourself and your love with others.

Fifty-eight

Listen to the great wisdom inside you. There is a voice inside you that is always speaking, yet it is perennially silent. It is the voice that speaks without speaking. It is the voice that moves you without moving. It is the voice that calls you to action and the voice that calls you to silence.

If you work for a corporation and you must get up in the morning and go do your nine to five, you risk this flow. I do not mean that you can't stay in your flow at your job, you can, as long as the doing the job is true to you. If doing the job is no longer true to you, that is where you find trouble and imbalance. You must be true to yourself.

The world has many options. The options will open when you listen and stay in tune with the quiet underlying river of life. Some options are good for you and some are not. Be discerning of what supports your true nature.

Fifty-nine

Take care of each other. You are not here just for yourself. You are here for love. Love your neighbor, love your village, love your community, love your world and do what is true to you.

You came here with a mission, a path, a directive from on high. You came here with an intention that is good and pure. You came here to love.

When you live your life as if it is lived for the highest good of humanity and the highest good of all, special things happen. Doors open, opportunities find you. Your way is shown.

You are right now on your path, whether you know it or not. It is under your feet.

Sixty

Use your power for the highest good. Stay out of harms way. When you are good, honest and true to yourself and others, good follows you everywhere. When you are good, honest and true to yourself and others, you spread love and so you are loved. When you are good, honest and true to yourself, you are full of self-respect and your self-esteem grows. This feels good on so many levels because love is expansive.

You are a multi-dimensional being. When you are true to yourself on this dimension you are true to yourself on all dimensions. You cannot separate it out. Then you are true to love.

Strength and Power

Sixty-one

Man, woman, male, female, yin and yang are the balance of opposites. The male is the active force and the female is the receptive force. The male takes action, the female listens and receives.

Each person has both male and female inside. Each person has the point of balance of opposites. This balance point is the Tao.

When you find the balance point inside yourself, you feel comfortable, happy and glad. When you are out of balance you feel unsettled.

When a city is in balance, the people are happy. When a country is in balance, all are cared for. When the earth is in balance you will know you have come home. When you have come home you are one with the universe. When you are one with the universe you are one with yourself.

Sixty-two

The Tao is the source of ten-thousand things. The Tao is the source of all things. The Tao is present all the time. The Tao does not judge. The Tao is.

When you are good and when you are happy, come to the Tao. When you are lost, come to the Tao. It's only one breath away. It only takes a moment to come home.

Sixty-three

Do nothing. Stay in the flow. This does not mean that you take no action. Take action that is aligned.

See greatness in little things. Watch the ant walk across the rose. He is very busy walking across the rose but he is taking his time. He is very present while he makes his trek across the great land of the flower petal. He doesn't worry if he will get to his destination. He simply goes forward, no matter what size his load. He is present.

Take each step gently. Walk forward with your heart open and your mind clear. Look for the simple in all things.

You have been taught that you must accomplish great deeds and make great money in order to be successful. This is not true to the sage. To the sage, you are successful when you touch the Tao. You are successful when you feel love. You are successful when you witness life.

Sixty-four

Peace is eternal. Come from peace.

A journey of a thousand miles starts with one step. One step, one step, one step. One step, one step, one step. Slowly, surely you place one foot in front of the other; in the same sure-footed manner that grandfather time clicks the clock, moment by moment.

One step, one step, one step, just like the rose opens her petals, one at a time.

Sixty-five

Look deeply. Look down inside the rose. See the center of the rose and the beauty that lives within. Inside your center is a similar beauty.

This is true for everyone, no matter where you live, no matter what you wear, no matter if you are dark skinned or light, no matter if you are rich or poor. The Tao does not discriminate. The Tao is eternal and it is inside each and every one of you.

If you understand that the Tao is inside everyone, how can you discriminate? If you understand that the Tao is eternal and everywhere, how would you lead? What kind of leader will you be? Will you recognize everyone as yourself? How long will it take you to know this? Only one moment, once you find the Tao.

Sixty-six

The sea is humble. It receives the blessings of the rivers of bounty. The river is humble. It receives the blessings of the streams of bounty. The streams are humble. They receive the blessings of the wellsprings of life.

Be like the water, be humble. Receive the blessings of life.

Be like the sage. Lead with humility and reverence for all of life. Recognize everyone as yourself and you will know what to do.

Sixty-seven

Be peaceful and peace will find you. Be peaceful and you will notice the peacefulness around you.

Stay in balance. Keep your body strong. Take care of yourself. Take care of your body. Eat well. Exercise moderately. Stay in balance.

Your body is your temple. When the body is strong and balanced it is easier to stay in touch with love.

Sixty-eight

Love translates into action. When you are connected to love, your actions are loving. The boss is supportive, the employee is satisfied. The husband is powerful and the wife is accomplished. The child is delighted, the elder is respected and honored. The clown makes you laugh and death helps you cry.

When you come from love, life is easier.

Think of a canoe and place the canoe upon the river. Place it in the middle of the stream where there are no rapids or boulders. In this place the canoe will travel by itself without a guide, staying in the middle of the flow.

If you take the canoe and you turn around and you try hard to go paddling upstream, you go nowhere. The river has its own course. You cannot really fight the river. Turn your boat around and go with the flow.

Sixty-nine

War, you want to talk about war? I want to talk about love. Why is there war? There is war because there is greed and fear. There is war because people don't know that they already have enough. There is war because people do not yet know the Tao.

Peace, you want to talk about peace? There is peace when there is no fear. When you, humanity, realize that the earth is temporary and yet the earth is endowed with richness for all, then there will be peace on earth. You will realize peace by connecting with the Tao. Where is the Tao? The Tao is everywhere. Where is the easiest place to find it? In your heart, of course.

Seventy

I am the Tao. I live inside you. I live inside all things. I am everywhere. I am eternal. There is no place where I am not.

Leave your mind behind. Touch your heart. There you will find me.

Seventy-one

Everything comes in cycles. In the spring the grass is fresh and green. The grass grows tall in the summer and in the fall it turns color. In the winter it dies.

The wind blows, the tree shimmers. The tide goes in and the tide goes out. What makes this happen? The Tao. Stay in touch with the cycles of life. Your path is right under your feet. Look no further than the soles of your own feet.

You say, "Oh, Lao Tzu, I should be further along. I should be richer, I should have children, I should be famous by now, and I should be stronger, healthier and more magnificent." I say, how can it be so, if this is what is? You are where you are. You are who you are. Can you be anywhere else? There is only one moment and that moment is right here, right now.

If you are sick or if you are well, take care of yourself. Do not deny the flesh. The flesh exists. Take care of the flesh. If you need money to function, get some money. Do what it takes to bring to you what you need. Take some action.

But also, remember to take some inaction!

Remember to be still so you can be guided. When you are still, nature will move you. You will attract to yourself all that you need. The Tao is not greedy, the Tao is very generous.

Seventy-two

There is great order in the Universe. When your life is in order, you feel connected to all things. You feel peaceful. When there is balance there is peace.

You say, "But, Lao Tzu, how can there be balance when some are rich and some are poor? How can there be balance when there is not fairness?"

Balance is inherent in all things. Without balance life would not exist at all. You live in duality. Here on earth, there is light and dark, good and bad, rich and poor, and within it, balance.

Take the bees. The bees serve the queen. The queen is not arrogant, she is just the queen. The bees are not subservient, they simply serve. Everyone has his or her role. Each role is necessary.

I am not saying the rich should get richer and the poor get poorer. I am saying balance is inherent. Balance is necessary for life to exist.

So can the world move up? Can consciousness evolve? Absolutely, and it will. Again I say, there is enough for all. Share. When you share and all are nourished you will feel good. And you will still be unique.

Seventy-three

The Tao is eternal. I have said this before. I will say it again. The Tao is eternal. Inside the Tao is love. Inside the Tao is balance. When you are in touch with the Tao you feel good and you are in the flow. When you lose touch with the Tao you get confused and you do not prosper.

Within the Tao you have choice. The Tao is the balance of opposites. You can choose one side or the other side and yet you choose the Tao. You can incarnate as a man or as a woman and you are still connected to the Tao.

You can walk a path of faith and virtue and feel the Tao. Or you can walk a path of war, out of touch with the Tao, but the Tao is still there.

Do not strive for material things, but take care of yourself. This is balance. Good things will come to you.

Eat well. Nourish your body, but do not stuff yourself. This is the Tao. Play, work, sleep, do your chores. You can do them in alignment with the Tao of love or out of alignment with the Tao of love. It's your choice. You already know which one makes you feel better. Your choice. I choose love. I choose the Tao.

Seventy-four

When you die, you live. There is no death. Though you will lose your body, you will find yourself there.

In society, there are rules. We must have rules to have order. If the rules are aligned with the Tao, the rules are guidelines and the rules will work. They are made by wise people.

A simple rule, do not kill each other. If this were followed there would be no war. There would be no need for weapons. There would be less fear. One simple rule, do not kill each other. Think about this; Why do you kill each other? You are not hungry for the other's flesh. You are simply threatened because you fear lack, when there isn't any, really.

Find your source inside yourself. Calm down and look inside. You will find the entire universe is there. Every answer you seek is inside you. Every prayer you have ever made is within you.

"But, oh, what about my prayers that haven't been answered?" I say, add one word. The word is yet. All prayers will be answered in God's timing. Keep your faith strong.

Seventy-five

You live in duality. You live in free will. You are free to act as you choose.

Your higher calling is to know we are all one. Your higher calling is to take care of yourself. Your higher calling is to take care of each other.

The systems are currently corrupt. These corrupt systems are falling down. As the systems fall apart there is chaos. You are living in the midst of great chaos. From chaos comes reform. From reform comes your higher calling.

Question: "What do you mean by reform?" I mean, renovated, reevaluated, recalled and reinstated.

Seventy-six

You are born pure and strong, simple and clean. You do bring your past memories with you. This is one long life that lasts for many lifetimes. You are there throughout time and space.

Life will carry you forward. When you get in the river of the Tao, there is a beautiful flow to life. When you take care of the body and keep it strong and flexible, the body gives back. When you are out of balance, the body is harder to carry around. When you are sick, it is more difficult to be in the flesh. Therefore, know that love lives inside you in every moment, in every condition. It is important to do the best you can to take good care of yourself and your body temple.

Eat well, take your greens, drink clear water, and take your vitamins and minerals. Pray with gratitude, live in moderation. Do not consume too much, but if you desire something enjoy yourself in moderation. This is the Tao. Do not put yourself down. Lift yourself up. Do not praise yourself. Be moderate, find the middle way. This is the Tao.

Seventy-seven

In the lower self, the rich get richer and the poor get poorer. This has been your story on earth throughout the dark ages.

Will you come out of the dark ages?

In your higher self, there is a balancing out. Those who have enough will share with those who do not.

Those who have more than enough will share with all of humanity.

We in heaven are waiting, watching and holding the pole for this dream to come true on earth.

Seventy-eight

Consider water. It flows through any pathway. It is not discriminating. It doesn't care what ground it moves across. It is flexible and yielding. Yet, it is strong enough to move a large stone and create its own pathway.

Be like the water, flexible, strong, undiscriminating, creating your own pathway.

How can you be both flexible and strong? Let's put it in ordinary terms. Do your yoga. Walk your walk. Create your pathway. Use moderation.

If you are a wise person and you are called to leadership, lead in this manner: Be strong, charismatic yet flexible and yielding. Be like the water. Do not discriminate against rich or poor. Love and cherish everyone.

Create programs so that all have opportunities. Educate the people. Make sure everyone is fed. This is reform.

Seventy-nine

It's time to balance out. Balance out on earth. It's time to share the resources with each other. It's time to share the wealth. Start with your neighbor and community. When more power is given, move to your state or your country. When more power is given, take on the world. Go where you are called to feed the people.

Your planet is not that big. It is big enough. It is full enough. It has enough for everyone. Inside duality you have rich and poor but you also have the great scales of justice. Rich and poor can be far more balanced than they are now. They do not need to be polar opposites. Come closer together. Look in each other's eyes. Love each other. Look at your neighbor and love him or her. Notice your neighbor's heart loving you.

Be kind to other people for your time will come. What you put forward you shall receive. Treat everyone as if they are yourself. This means, treat everyone as you want to be treated, because you will be treated how you treat everyone. It's universal law. Wake up. Wake up now. We are all one.

Eighty

The simple life is the best life. Move toward simplicity. Do you remember riding a horse to work or to school? Imagine how fun that would be.

Surely technology can be used for good. If you use your technology to share education, to simplify life and to feed the people, then this is using technology for good.

Find the balance again. Find the balance of simplicity and love, the balance of caring for each other and using your sciences.

Imagine a beautiful scale of justice. Place one stone on one side and one stone of the same size on the other. They balance perfectly. Imagine an old rusty scale with a pile of stones piled high on one side and a pile of stones piled high on the other side. Which one is more appealing?

Eighty-one

Love is the answer. Love is the key. Love is the answer to every question you ask. Try asking a few questions and answering them all with love. Think of a few people and think of them with love. Consider your world and consider it with love.

Consider your death and consider it with love. What do you want your legend to be? How about love?

About the Author

Dawn Lianna is a teacher, counselor and clear intuitive. She holds her Master's degree in counseling and psychology and is a Master NLP trainer. She teaches communication skills online through Education 2 go, the largest online university in the country.

Dawn has a deep commitment to consciousness, right action and helping humanity awaken to love. Her profound skills to see to the root cause of an issue are balanced with a deep and gentle nature. The insightful and simple teachings that flow through her help people find inner peace in their daily lives.

You can access her other book, Lao Tzu Now, her CD's, courses and free resources at her website www.intuitivecallings.com.

CPSIA information can be obtained at www.ICGtesting.com
Printed in the USA
BVOW011650200513

321183BV00004B/14/P